Four Seasons
in the Woods

WRITTEN AND ILLUSTRATED BY Henry B. Kane

 ALFRED · A · KNOPF

NEW YORK / 1968

For Derek . . .
whose father learned early
to know the woods and
those who live there

This is a Borzoi Book published by Alfred A. Knopf, Inc.

Copyright © 1968 by Henry B. Kane
All rights reserved under International and Pan-American Copyright
Conventions. Published in the United States by Alfred A. Knopf, Inc.,
New York, and simultaneously in Canada by Random House of Canada
Limited, Toronto. Distributed by Random House, Inc., New York.
Library of Congress Catalog Card Number: 68-15324
Manufactured in the United States of America

Screech Owl (frontis)
Squirrel Tracks (opposite)

CO. SCHOOLS
C723772

Winter

...the Time

Snowflakes

# of Snow

All day long it had been snowing. Softly the
flakes sifted down through the pines, the
hemlocks, and the leafless oaks. In early evening
the storm ended. A full moon shone down on
a new, clean blanket of white.

White-footed Mouse
Tracks

Now the creatures of the night appeared. White-footed mice played across the snow. They leaped and danced without a care. And they searched for new-fallen seeds on the soft surface.

Cottontail rabbits nibbled the tips of twigs pulled down by the weight of the snow. They also gnawed the thin bark of small trees.

Now, too, came the hunters.

White-footed Mouse

*Cottontail
and Red Fox*

A cottontail crouched under the snow-covered branches of a hemlock. Its nose twitched and its ears were alert to catch the slightest sound.

But the soft snow muffled the approach of a hunting fox. His searching nose caught the scent of the hidden rabbit. Slowly and carefully he crept forward. Then, swiftly, he pounced. The cottontail leaped wildly, but too late.

A saw-whet owl perched in the lower branches of a pine. Smallest of all eastern owls, he was no bigger than a robin. He had come down from his ice-bound, north-woods home in search of an easier living. Below him the mice raced and leaped across the sparkling white surface. Suddenly, on silent wings, the little owl swooped down. All but one of the players escaped into hiding.

The lives of mice and rabbits are short, but so are their memories. Before long the white-footed mice were back at play, and the cottontails nibbled again at twigs and buds.

Saw-whet Owl

With the first light of day, some of the mice retired to tree holes. Others had snug nests in an old stone wall.

The owl went to sleep in a dead oak stub. And the fox curled up for a nap at the foot of a big boulder.

The harsh call of a crow and the scream of blue jays greeted the dawn. The voices of the winter woods are those of birds.

A brown creeper hitched his way up the trunk of a pine. He went around and around as though he were climbing a spiral staircase. With his curved bill he probed the rough bark for insects and their eggs. He climbed only as far as the first branches. Then he flew to the base of another pine and started all over again.

Brown Creeper

White-breasted Nuthatch

A flock of chickadees searched through the low growth. They swung upside down to examine the undersides of branches. They peered into cracks and crevices. They pried under loose bark. Their hunt for food is never-ending. And all the while they kept up a cheery chatter of "chick-a-dee-dee-dee, chick-a-dee-dee-dee."

There were other bird voices. As the brown creeper went up a pine he met another searcher coming down headfirst. With a harsh "yank, yank" the surprised nuthatch flew across to another tree.

Tiny, golden-crowned kinglets flitted through the thick branches of firs and hemlocks. They called "see-see-see" to one another. And now and then came the rattle of a hairy woodpecker, or the rapid "tchee-tchee-tchee" of its look-alike small brother, a downy woodpecker. The birds of winter are not singers. Rather, they are talkers.

Chickadee

Not all those who live in the woods were awake and stirring. Some slept the whole winter through. In their dens, under the old stone wall, lay chipmunks and woodchucks. Curled up in balls, they hardly breathed. They were hibernating, and would sleep until spring returned.

Raccoons and skunks were sleeping, too, but not as soundly. On mild nights in midwinter they woke and went outside to stretch their legs.

Most insects died with the first frosts. They left eggs and pupa to carry their kind through winter. But there were those who hibernated. A January thaw woke mourning cloak butterflies who fluttered briefly through the aisles of the woods. Beneath the snow, a rotted log was host to a varied collection of sleepers. There was a queen hornet, several sow bugs, millepedes curled up like pin wheels, centipedes, and a number of beetles. They were cold, but not frozen, and would wake again.

Pill
Bug

Sow
Bugs

Hornet
Queen

Ground
Beetle

Millipede

Some trees, evergreens such as pines, have leaves or needles all year long. Others are deciduous, losing their leaves in autumn and growing new ones in the spring. The buds from which these new leaves would come were formed the year before. Now, in winter, protected by hard caps from cold and ice, they wait for warmer days. Then they will burst open. Those long, skeleton twigs and branches will again be covered with a thick cloak of green.

White Birch Buds

*White-footed
Mouse*

A gray squirrel hopped slowly across the snow. His tracks looked much like those of a white-footed mouse, only larger; or a cottontail, only smaller. In autumn he had hidden acorns here and there under leaves and top earth. Now he was hunting them out. The squirrel moved slowly with his head down. He stopped, as though his sniffing nose had located a nut. Down through the snow he dug, but no acorn. He tried another spot. Still no acorn. The third try was successful.

No squirrel can locate all the nuts he buries. Many trees sprout from his lost treasures. A snowshoed boy and his dog came through the woods. They sent the squirrel scampering up a snow-free dead birch. At the same time a dark shadow slipped away from the top of a pine. A great horned owl had left her nest.

*Gray
Squirrel*

Cottontail

Gray Squirrel

Great Horned Owl

13

The days grew longer and warmer, and slowly the snows melted. In open spaces, ground pine and club moss appeared. They had stayed alive and green all winter under the white cover. Red partridge berries like little eyes peeked out from under matted leaves.

Overhead, tree buds swelled. The twigs of swamp maples turned red as their buds waited to burst open. New growth at the tips of pines, hemlocks, and firs were ready to push off their thin protecting caps.

After long months of ice and snow, the woods were at the edge of spring.

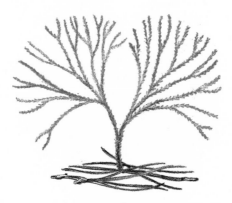

Ground Pine

Columbine

Spring

Dogwood Blossoms

...the Time of New Life

Soft spring rains soon washed away the snows
of winter. Everywhere life began again. The sun
reached down through bare branches. Spring
flowers pushed up from the warming earth.
Hibernating animals and insects awoke from their
long sleep. Young animals were born in hidden
dens and tree holes. Summer birds returned from
the south and the nesting season began.

When ferns unfolded their tightly-curled fiddle-heads, the first young animals appeared. A pair of white-footed mice had taken over an old catbird's nest. They roofed it over, and now it was home to five baby mice. They grew fast. One warm night the young white-feet came out to see the world. They clambered down from their home and explored the floor of the woods. They were gray above, not reddish-brown like their parents. But all had white underparts and the white feet that gave them their name.

Baby cottontails were abroad both day and night. They hopped across the pine carpet, and nibbled at new green shoots. Their noses wiggled constantly, and their ears turned in every direction. The slightest alarm set them scampering into hiding. A flash of white from their little cottony tails, and they were gone.

Young Cottontail Rabbits

The first spring flowers hardly looked like flowers. Skunk cabbages grew along a wandering brook. Their green and purple hoods had weathered the ice and snow of winter. In each one, almost hidden from sight, was an oval spike. Even before the warmth of spring had reached inside, they were covered with tiny yellow blossoms. Now early bees and wasps came to visit. No flowers are hidden from them.

In late March fuzzy hepatica buds pushed through last year's rusty leaves. Their flowers seemed too fragile for this early season. Violets soon followed. In sunlit spots birdfoot violets looked up at the clear blue skies above.

Skunk Cabbage

Birdfoot Violets

There were other violets: white, yellow, and all shades of blue. Along with them came more spring flowers in quick succession. Delicate wood and rue-anemones, showy white bloodroot blossoms, and stately Jack-in-the-pulpits all came into bloom. In some places the shiny green leaves and foamy white flowers of Canada mayflowers carpeted the woodland floor. Here and there were clumps of trailing arbutus, their blossoms pink and wonderfully fragrant. Painted trilliums lifted their white, pink-lined petals above their spreading leaves.

There were spring-beauties, starflowers, May-apples, many more. Each passing day brought something new. But spring reached its peak when the beautiful nodding blossoms of the lady's-slippers appeared.

Painted Trilliums

lady's-slippers

*Hairy
Woodpecker*

Somewhere a woodpecker hammered on a dead stub. He was not hunting for food in the rotted wood. He just seemed to enjoy the sound, like a boy with a drum.

High overhead two young horned owls moved restlessly about their nest. They did not lack food. A dead crow and a skunk were there to satisfy

Fledgling Blue Jay

24

their hunger. The birds were still covered with fluffy white down, but their wing feathers were growing fast. Before long they would be trying them out.

In a bulky nest in another pine, fledgling crows called impatiently for food. Growing birds are always hungry, but young crows make more noise about it than most.

A pair of blue jays slipped quietly in and out of the thick lower branches of a spruce. In a well-hidden nest, their family of four was growing fast. Soon they would leave the nest and fly noisily through the woods after their parents.

For weeks the drumming of a cock grouse had sounded through the woods. Standing erect on an old log, he beat his wings against the air. Starting slowly, at first there were a few thumps. Then his wings moved faster and faster. They made a muffled roar like distant thunder. Suddenly he stopped and the woods were still. Minutes went by; then the thunder came again.

In mid-May the spiked scarlet flowers of columbine nodded on rocky slopes. By this time the drumming had almost stopped. While the cock was being noisy, his mate had been sitting quietly on her ten pale brown eggs. When they hatched she would not have to feed her young. They would leave the nest soon after hatching. All summer long she would lead them through the woods. And like barnyard chicks, they would scratch for their own seeds and catch their own insects.

*Hen Grouse
on Nest*

27

By late spring, young birds and animals were
everywhere. There were families of raccoons
and foxes, owls, crows, chickadees, and many more.

At night a family of skunks trailed across the
pine needles. The young were small copies of
their mother. They had broad white patches on
their coal-black backs. And like hers, their tails
were tipped with white.

The mother skunk was in the lead, and her
young waddled along behind in single file. When
she stopped at a good hunting ground, they
tumbled over one another in play. With her nose,

she rooted under pine needles and dead leaves. Insects, grubs, and worms were living there. The young skunks pounced on them hungrily. They were never at a loss for food.

Bright-eyed red squirrels scampered through the trees. When they first emerged from their tree-hole home, they had been timid and cautious. For a time they clung tightly to the rough bark outside its entrance. Then they began to climb, slowly and carefully at first. They stretched their legs and strengthened all their muscles.

It did not take long. Soon they were chasing up and down tree trunks. They moved so fast their feet hardly seemed to touch the bark. They raced through the upper branches. They leaped wildly from tree to tree. They shared the woods' upper story with the birds. It was their natural home.

Young Skunks

29

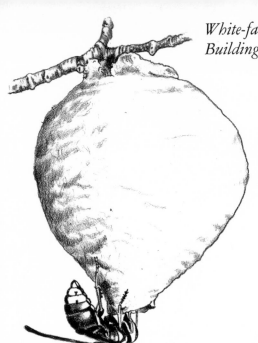

*White-faced Hornet Queen
Building New Nest*

With the first warm days of spring, queen bees and hornets came out of hibernation. One hornet started a small paper nest on a maple twig. In it she laid a few eggs and raised the first brood of workers. They would take over enlarging the nest and rearing more workers. She would stay inside laying more eggs. By midsummer there would be thousands of hornets in a nest as big as a watermelon.

When the dogwoods bloomed the first of the big, night-flying moths appeared. A female Cecropia, her red-and-white body heavy with eggs, clung to the bark of a birch tree. After she had mated she would fly slowly from tree to tree. Her eggs would be laid on the leaves of cherry, maple, and other trees. In a week or two a new generation of Cecropia caterpillars would hatch.

Cecropia Moth

And so life returned to the woods. The cold, dark days of sleep had given way to a time for awakening, for rebirth. New flowers, new birds, new animals and insects arrived in a rush.

Now the hurried days of spring were over. They would be followed by a quieter time, a time for growing up.

Young Crow

*Young
Red Fox*

Summer

...the

Lady's-tresses / Pipsissewa / Wintergreen

Time of Heat

On a summer morning the woods had awakened
to the calls of jays, flickers, veerys, and other
birds. The cool of night had lasted well through
the morning. Now, at midday, the woods were
still. Heat had settled down, and only the top-
most branches of the tallest trees stirred.

On the forest floor there was a breathless hush.
Nothing moved. Even the bell-like flowers of the
shinleaf hung motionless.

Partridgeberry / Shinleaf

Cecropia
Caterpillar

Few insects are bothered by midsummer heat. In fact, most of them thrive on it. One such was a Cecropia caterpillar, as big as a man's forefinger. Many weeks had passed since it left the egg. Ever since, it had feasted on the leaves of a cherry tree near the edge of the woods. It had outgrown several skins, shedding each in turn for a new and more comfortable one.

Now full-grown, the caterpillar was the color of the leaves on which it fed. Shiny knobs of yellow, red, and black lined its back and sides. At last it stopped eating and became restless.

For some time the big green caterpillar wandered up and down the cherry tree. Then it began to weave its cocoon.

Cecropia
Cocoon

Inside a cover of leaves the caterpillar spun itself a home. From its mouth came a thin, shiny thread of pure silk. As its head moved up and down, back and forth, it glued the turns of the thread down firmly. Its body pressed them tight together. At last they were packed into a hard, smooth chamber.

A few days later, a marvelous change occurred. Inside the cocoon, the caterpillar's skin split at the head. By wriggling and squirming, the loose skin was pushed off completely. There, in place of the green caterpillar, was a dark brown object. It was a pupa, third stage in the life of a moth.

When another spring came, a moth would emerge from the pupa. It would push out of the cocoon. Then, when its wings had grown strong, it would be ready to fly; a Cecropia, biggest moth in the woods.

Cecropia
Pupa

*Inchworm on
Cedar Twig*

Some insects such as Cecropia caterpillars are bright and colorful. Others are almost impossible to see. There are several kinds of inchworms in the woods, all caterpillars of geometrid moths. Those that feed on cedar tips look like dead cedar twigs. When they are at rest they stand stiff and straight. Another kind feeds on hickory leaves and has markings like hickory twigs. It is their protection against insect eaters.

Moths, too, often have protective coloration. Some have bright colors on their underwings. But, when they are at rest on rough bark, their fore-wings cover the underwings. Then they almost disappear from sight.

There are many ways of escaping the notice of enemies. Camouflage is one of the most effective. It is also one of the most common, especially among insects.

*Moth on
Cedar Bark*

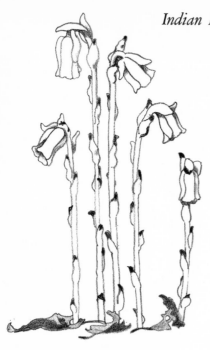

It is the hush of midday. An unseen hawk screams from the sky above. But, for the most part, the woods are left to the quiet insects, the ferns, and the flowers.

Among the strangest of summer flowers are the Indian pipes. They grow in small clumps, white and waxy. The green color of other plants comes from their chlorophyll. But Indian pipes have no chlorophyll. Their nourishment comes from the decayed leaves on which they grow. Yet they are true flowering plants, not fungi like mushrooms.

Many plants have unexpected relatives. It is not surprising to find that the bright orange wood lilies are in the same family as tulips. But it does seem peculiar to think of them also as closely related to asparagus, which they are.

Wood Lily

*Gray Birch Stub
with Bracket Fungus*

The stub of a dead birch stood at the edge of the woods. It was rotted and weak, and leaned dangerously. Near its top was a hole, entrance to a white-footed mouse's home. It was broad daylight, and the homeowner was asleep inside.

A sparrow hawk hunted across a nearby field. Now and then he stopped in midair, hovering low over the grass tops. Coming to the edge of the woods, he lit on the top of the dead birch.

Sparrow hawks are the smallest of American hawks. They live on mice and insects, only rarely birds. Now he called a shrill "kee-kee." The suddenly awakened mouse panicked. Rushing to his doorway, he leaped wildly into space. But he was not quick enough to escape the little hawk. They hit the pine needles together.

Moments later, the hunter flew up into a pine with his prey. He looked around alertly, then screamed a victorious "kee-kee, kee-kee."

The tree hole had lost its tenant.

*Sparrow Hawk with
White-footed Mouse*

A mushroom is a fungus. It has no chlorophyll or leaf green of its own. It grows mostly on dead wood or leaves, and gets its food from them.

In late summer, mushrooms suddenly appeared everywhere. Some were almost too tiny to see. Others were as big as dinner plates. They came in all shapes, sizes, and colors. They grew on fallen logs and tree trunks, from the ground, and on mossy banks. Many were beautiful and could not be overlooked. Some were very good to eat. And a few were deadly poison.

Mushrooms can hardly be missed. But some of the creatures that moved among them were seldom seen. They were small and often stayed hidden.

*Gray
Tree Frog*

There were frogs in the
woods. Hunting across the forest
floor were beautiful, brown
wood frogs with dark masks.
They were the color of the dead
leaves and pine needles through
which they searched.

Tree frogs climbed through shrubs and low
bushes. Usually they were a shade of gray, but
they could also change to brown and green. Like
their small cousins, the spring peepers, they had
sticky toes. When they leaped after insects, their
toes held firmly to the first thing they touched.

In times past there had been dangerous snakes
in these woods. In their place now were timid
ring-necked and DeKay snakes. They were pencil-
thin, and only a foot or so long. Garter snakes
and black snakes usually kept to the edge of the
woods. They found hunting better in nearby
fields and meadows.

Along the brook where the earth was always
wet, lived newts and salamanders. They were
seldom seen in the open. But turning over a

*Ring-necked
Snake*

*DeKay
Snake*

stone or rotting log was apt to surprise one or more of them. It might be a little red newt or a red-backed salamander. Or it might be a much bigger spotted salamander, shiny black with yellow spots. No matter which, it would quickly wriggle away to another hiding place.

All of these shy little creatures helped to keep down the insect population. At the end of summer they would start their long winter's sleep. And in spring, when new insects appeared, they would wake to greet them, alert and hungry.

Spotted Salamander

Autumn

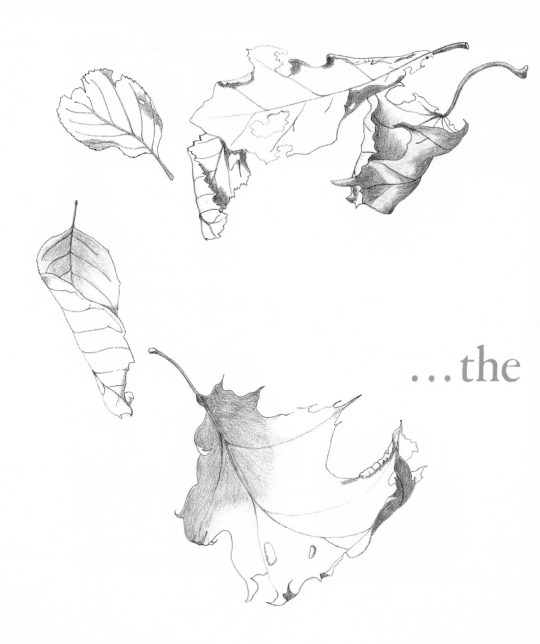

...the

Woodland Leaves

Time of Falling Leaves

The days grew shorter and the nights grew cooler. Warblers, blackbirds, grackles, and other birds gathered together. They moved southward in flocks. Some stopped briefly to feed. For a short time the woods were full of color and movement. Then the migrating birds were gone.

The long, hot days of summer were over. Autumn had come.

In early spring, spicebushes had been yellow bouquets. Now their scarlet berries gleamed brightly along the brook. A spring peeper searched among them for late insects. Soon the insects would be gone. Then the little tree frog would burrow under soft moss or dead leaves. If all went well, he would wake early next spring. Of all the frogs, his shrill voice would be the first to greet its arrival.

With the coming of autumn, the green leaves of summer changed color. Maples turned brilliant red, yellow, and orange. Birches and hickories were dressed in bright yellow. Beech leaves were a rich brown. Oaks turned scarlet or brown.

*Fallen Leaves
on a Woods Pool*

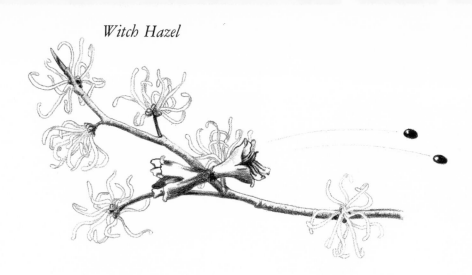

Few places are as colorful as our woods in autumn. But their beauty is short-lived. Soon the leaves lose their hold. A passing breeze sends them down in showers. For a brief moment the woods are floored with a brilliant carpet. Then the fallen leaves turn dry and brown.

Witch hazel leaves had fallen before their blossoms appeared. They were the last flowers of the season, twisting yellow ribbons. Old seed pods dried and shot out shiny brown seeds.

Bittersweet vines climbed high into some trees. They carried clusters of orange seed pods. The first frosts burst them open to reveal bright scarlet fruit. Not all the woods' color died with its leaves.

Bittersweet

The camouflage of any creature is good only against the right background. A brown weasel is hard to see on brown pine needles. But against white snow it stands out clearly. So, as the autumn days grew cooler, the weasels changed their coats. Brown hairs were shed and white ones took their place. Only the tips of their tails were still black. That tip would be the one thing seen by a hunting owl or fox. When the attack came, its owner would already be disappearing under the snow.

Raccoons were awake through most of the autumn. But, with cold weather, they grew sleepier and sleepier. They would spend the coldest months sound asleep in their tree-hole homes. Neither biting winds nor swirling snows would bother them there.

Longtail Weasels

Winter

Summer

It was night, a cold night. A screech owl perched in a small pine tree. He watched and listened for movement below. When a noise came from behind he quickly turned his head around. He was looking right straight down the middle of his back.

Then the owl gave its call. It was by no means a screech. Rather, it was a mournful wail. Many years ago, a man named Thoreau lived in nearby woods. He said it sounded like, "Oh-o-o-o that I had never been bor-or-or-or-orn."

Near by, a furry redback mouse nibbled on fallen seeds. He heard that sad call and knew that danger threatened. Without a moment's hesitation, he quickly scurried into hiding, not making a sound.

Redbacked Mouse

The year was nearing its end. It had started with snow and ice. Then the sun climbed higher and higher. The snows melted and spring flowers bloomed. Frogs and toads sang or croaked from every pool and brook. Birds returned from the south and sleeping animals awoke. Young creatures of all sorts were born or hatched.

Then came summer, the time of heat. It was a period of rest after the rush of spring.

And now it was autumn, spring in reverse. Birds returned to the south. Animals went back to sleep. Trees were bare once again. At last, with the first falling flakes of snow, the year had come full circle.

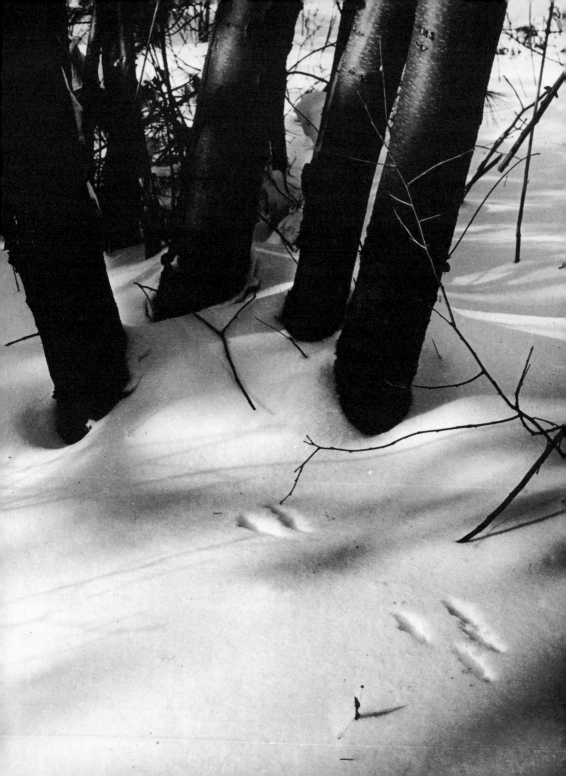

All night long it had been snowing. With the
dawn, squirrels raced over the white surface.
Juncos and tree sparrows, migrants from the north,
hunted across it for seeds. But under that soft
blanket lay plants and animals; insects, frogs,
and many more. Most of those who lived in the
woods were deep in sleep.

The four seasons have no end and no
beginning. There are new actors, but they play
the same parts. There are new stage sets, but they
look like those that went before. It is a play that
never ends. It is full of life and beauty. But most
of all, it is full of surprises.

Juncos

*Black Birches
and Squirrel Tracks*

INDEX